NO-COOK COOKERY

Ting and Neil Morris

Illustrated by Ruth Levy

W
FRANKLIN WATTS

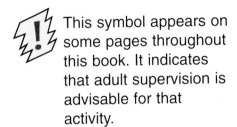

This symbol appears on some pages throughout this book. It indicates that adult supervision is advisable for that activity.

This edition published in 2004 by
Franklin Watts
96 Leonard Street
London
EC2A 4XD

Franklin Watts Australia
45-51 Huntley Street
Alexandria
NSW 2015

Cover design: Alice Young
Editor: Hazel Poole
Consultant: David Lambert
Designer: Sally Boothroyd
Photography: John Butcher
Artwork: Ruth Levy / Joanne Cowne
Models: Emma Morris
Picture Research: Ambreen Husain

ISBN 0 7496 5912 2

A CIP catalogue record is available for this book at the British Library.

Contents

Introduction

In this book you can learn something about food both by reading about it and by having fun with simple cooking. The information in the fact boxes will tell you about different foods – where they come from, how they are grown and processed, and their importance in customs and festivals around the world.

We call it "no-cook cooking" because you will not be baking, frying or using the oven. Instead, you will be having fun measuring, stirring, mixing, rolling and decorating, with results that look and taste good! Some of the activities involve heating, cutting and peeling, so please always make sure that an adult is there to help you.

At the end of the book there is information on how food gives us energy, and the importance of a balanced diet.

But now you can get your fingers sticky – following simple recipes and making delicious things to eat, as you read about food.

Equipment and ingredients

The recipes in this book provide an introduction to cookery and need little adult help. Cooking activities that involve using heat or sharp knives are all specially marked. Always read the recipe through before you start, to make sure that you have all the necessary equipment and ingredients. You won't always have to weigh things, as the weight is usually printed on the pack that the food comes in. To make things easy, small amounts are given in level tablespoons: 2 tablespoons = 25 grams.

When you are ready to start, put on an apron, wash your hands and get together all the equipment and ingredients you will need. If you follow the instructions carefully, the results will be mouthwatering and fun – and when you've finished, don't forget to wash up and tidy everything away!

In this book the following equipment and ingredients are used:

EQUIPMENT
baking tin
bowls
brush (for glue)
cake board
cake cases
card
cellophane
cereal packet (empty)
chocolate box (empty)
chopping board
cling film
cocktail sticks
coloured paper
forks
glass jug
grater
greaseproof paper
ice-cream tub (large)
ice tray
icing bag and nozzle
jug
knife
lables
ladle
lolly moulds
lolly sticks
mixing bowl
muslin cloth
old magazines
palette knife

paper (coloured paper;
  tissue paper; wrapping
  paper)
petit-four cases
plastic bag
plastic bowl
plate
PVA glue
ribbon
rolling pin
saucepan
scissors
screw-top jar
sieve
silver foil
skewers
small pots
spoons
sweet wrappers
weights
whisk
wire rack
wooden spoon
INGREDIENTS
almond chips
almond essence
apple juice
blackcurrant juice
bran
bread (brown;
  white; bridge rolls;

French loaf; crusty rolls)
butter
cheese (cream cheese;
  curd cheese; processed
  cheese)
chocolate strands
cocoa powder
concentrated lemon juice
condensed milk
cooking chocolate
desiccated coconut
dried apricots
eggs
fizzy water
food colourings
fruit (apples; bananas;
  lemons; limes; oranges;
  pawpaw; pineapple;
  strawberries; tomatoes)
ginger ale
ground almonds
ice cubes
jam
Madeira cake
margarine
milk
mint leaves
nuts (almonds; cashews;
  hazelnuts)
nut oil
oats (jumbo and regular)
orange squash

parsley
quark
raisins
rye flakes
shredded wheat
soft margarine
soya milk
strawberry cordial
sugar (brown;
  caster; white;
  vanilla; icing)
sugar balls
sultanas
sunflower seeds
sweets (strawberry
  laces; liquorice; jelly
  beans)
Swiss rolls
vanilla essence
vegetables (carrots;
  celery; cucumber;
  lettuce)
water
wheat flakes
wheatmeal biscuits
whipping cream
yeast extract
yoghurt

A Healthy Start

Here's how to start your day with a bowl of healthy muesli.

YOU WILL NEED:
- large mixing bowl
- big screw-top jar
- 250 g jumbo oats
- 250 g regular oats
- 250 g wheat flakes
- 250 g rye flakes
- 2 tablespoons brown sugar
- 100 g sunflower seeds
- 100 g bran (optional)
- 300 g raisins and sultanas
- knife
- 125 g dried apricots
- chopping board
- label
- 250 g mixed hazelnuts, almonds and cashew nuts
- milk, yoghurt or fruit juice (to serve)

1 Put the oats and flakes in a large mixing bowl. (If you don't have the different types of flakes, use ordinary porridge oats to make up the quantities.) Add the brown sugar and sunflower seeds, and the bran.

2 Cut the raisins, sultanas and apricots into small pieces. Ask an adult to help you chop up the nuts. Put the fruit and nuts into the bowl and mix all the ingredients together.

3 Put the mixed muesli into the jar and screw the lid on tight. Label the jar, adding the date, and store it in a cool place.

4 Serve your muesli with milk, yoghurt, soya milk or fresh fruit juice.

5 On cold days you could add the milk or juice and heat the muesli up for five minutes. This will make a nice warm start to the day.

Cereals

Cereals are grasses that produce edible grains, which are the seeds of the plant. These grasses include wheat, oats, rice, maize, barley, millet, sorghum and rye. They are the most important plant foods in the world, and form a major part of most people's diet.

Cereals give us energy as well as protein, fibre, vitamins and minerals. Oats come originally from central Europe and are the major ingredient in the original Swiss muesli. They are widely grown in Europe and North America because they are suited to more types of different soils and climates than most cereals. Oats are easy to eat and have a rich, creamy flavour. The Swiss-German word *Müsli* comes from *Mus*, meaning mush or purée. This has become a popular breakfast cereal, because the ingredients are less processed than in other packaged cereals. Our muesli is also made with wheat flakes – whole grains of wheat that have been flattened between rollers – and bran, which is the outer protective layer of the grain.

When you get near the bottom of the jar, it's time to make another week's supply of muesli. For variety, add your own selection of fruit, nuts and seeds.

Cheese Boats

1 To sail a fleet of small boats on a sea of lettuce, first split the bridge rolls in half lengthways. Spread with margarine and a tiny amount of yeast extract. To make sails, cut the cheese slices into triangles and push cocktail sticks through them and into the rolls. You could add buoys by decorating cocktail sticks with colourful paper triangles and pushing the sticks into small tomatoes. Then arrange the boats and buoys on a crunchy lettuce sea.

2 Stay at sea with French bread submarines and a luxury sandwich liner. Mix the curd cheese and cream cheese together, and beat the mixture until it is smooth and fluffy.

3 Slice the banana and sprinkle it with lemon juice to stop it going brown. Then mash it up with a fork. Blend 4 tablespoons of sugar and one teaspoon of vanilla sugar into the basic cheese mixture. Add the banana, finely chopped almonds and a teaspoon of fresh orange juice.

4 Cut a small French loaf down the middle lengthways, and hollow the two halves out. Stuff one half with cheese spread and put the other half on top. Use two hollowed-out crusty rolls filled with spread to go with the big submarine. Wrapped in aluminium foil, these submarines are ideal for taking on picnics.

5 You can use the remaining spread on your luxury liner. Cut the crusts off the sliced brown and white bread. Fill two brown sandwiches and one white sandwich with cheese spread.

6 Cut one brown sandwich into an oblong hull, and keep the cut-off strip for a funnel. Cut the other brown sandwich into triangles, to make the bow and stern of the ship, and place them in position.

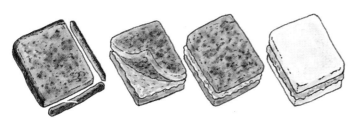

Now you can launch all your boats and have a cheese feast!

7 Cut the white sandwich into four squares, and use three of them to make the upper part of the ship. Cut a funnel from the fourth, and put the white and brown funnels in place.

Cheese

It is not known for sure when or where cheese was first made. According to one legend, an Arab merchant tasted some milk that had curdled in a goatskin bag. He liked the taste and a new food was discovered! We do know that Greek and Roman scholars wrote about cheese over 2,000 years ago.

Cheese is made from curdled milk, by separating the curd from the liquid whey. The curd is then pressed in a mould and allowed to ripen. The original milk usually comes from cows, goats or sheep, but in parts of Asia the milk of camels and water buffalo is also used. France produces the widest range of cheeses in the world, and many villages have their own speciality. Camembert, a famous rich creamy cheese, comes originally from the village of that name in Normandy. Roquefort is named after a village in southern France. This strong cheese is made from sheep's milk and is matured in local caves.

Coconut Bars

YOU WILL NEED:
- ✔ 20 cm square baking tin
- ✔ greaseproof paper   ✔ ribbon
- ✔ 500 g icing sugar   ✔ bowl
- ✔ 400 g can condensed milk
- ✔ 350 g desiccated coconut
- ✔ red food colouring   ✔ sieve
- ✔ strawberry laces   ✔ knife
- ✔ cellophane   ✔ metal spoon
- ✔ wooden spoon

1 Sift the icing sugar into a bowl, and mix it with the condensed milk. Then stir in the desiccated coconut with a wooden spoon. This will take a lot of strength, because the mixture is very stiff!

2 Line the base of a baking tin with greaseproof paper, and dust it with icing sugar. Put half of the mixture into the tin, pressing it down firmly with the back of a spoon.

3 Add a few drops of red food colouring to the rest of the mixture. Put only two or three drops in to start with, kneading the mixture carefully. Then press the pink mixture on top of the white mixture in the tin.

4 Leave the mixture to set for at least 12 hours. Then cut it into eight bars. Put strawberry laces around each bar, and then wrap them in cellophane. Tie the ends with ribbon.

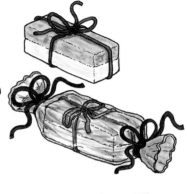

10

Coconut bars make a delicious snack and will keep for a month in an airtight container.

Coconuts

Coconuts are the fruit of the coconut palm. In the 15th century, Portuguese sailors thought the undeveloped buds on the outer husk of this huge nut looked rather like a face. So they called the nut *coco*, the Portuguese for "grimace". The husk cushions the inner seed when the coconut falls from the tree. Inside is a layer of thick white "meat", and the hollow centre is filled with a watery liquid called coconut milk. This makes a refreshing drink. The coconut palm grows up to 30 metres tall and is crowned with long, feathery leaves. One tree can produce about 50 coconuts each year and the largest coconuts in the world can weigh up to 18 kg each. These are harvested by climbing the tree and cutting off a cluster of nuts, or by gathering fallen nuts on the ground. The Philippines, Indonesia and Sri Lanka are the world's leading coconut producers.

Caribbean Tub

You will need a sharp knife to prepare the fruit for this tub. Ask an adult to help you.

1 Lay the pineapple on its side and cut off the top and bottom. Then cut the pineapple widthways into 2-cm slices. Cut the skin off each slice, and remove all the tiny black 'eyes', as well as the core in the middle. Then cut the slices into chunks and put them in the tub.

2 With a knife, score the orange into quarters and peel off the skin and pith. Cut the orange flesh into slices, quarter them and add them to the tub.

3 Cut the pawpaw in half lengthways. Scoop out the seeds and throw them away. Peel the pawpaw, cut it up into small pieces and put them in the tub.

4 Peel the banana, brush it with a little lime juice, slice it and put the slices in the tub.

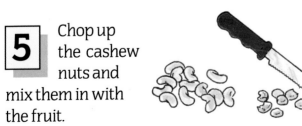

5 Chop up the cashew nuts and mix them in with the fruit.

Bananas

The banana plant first grew in India and south-east Asia. Arab traders took bananas to Africa. Then Portuguese explorers took roots of the plant, and its African name – *banana* – to the Canary Islands. From there it was taken across the Atlantic to the Caribbean and Central America. In recent years bananas have become very popular, especially in Europe. The big countries of Brazil, India and China are the world's largest banana producers. But small nations such as the Caribbean islands of St Lucia and Dominica depend on bananas and coconuts for their survival. Bananas are not easy to trade in because they cannot be stored. They must be harvested while they are still green, shipped to other countries and then delivered to shops – all within 10 to 20 days so that they are ripe and ready to eat. If you want to know where your bananas come from, look at the small label showing their country of origin.

6 Pour a tablespoon of lime juice and a teaspoon of nut oil all over the salad. Put the lid on the tub and shake it. Then keep it in the fridge until it's needed – your Caribbean fruit salad is perfect for packed lunches and picnics.

Thirst Quenchers

Herbal teas are good for you, and they are very thirst-quenching. All you need for your tea party are a teapot, strainer, spoons, cups and boiling water. Always ask an adult to pour on the boiling water. We've also added a strawberry punch for thirsty friends.

1 Pick a handful of mint leaves, and wash and crush them. Put the mint into a teapot and pour on boiling water. Strain the tea after four minutes, and when it is cool, pour it into a glass jug.

2 Add the juice of half a lemon, half an orange, some grated lemon and orange peel, and the sugar. Mix well and then chill.

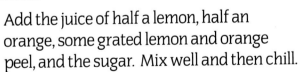

3 When you are ready to serve the mint tea, add the ginger ale and ice cubes. Put a thin slice of lemon or orange and a sprig of fresh mint into each glass.

Strawberry punch

YOU WILL NEED:
- ✔ large bowl
- ✔ ladle
- ✔ 100 g sugar
- ✔ 500 g strawberries (fresh or frozen)
- ✔ 100 ml apple juice
- ✔ 1 large lemon
- ✔ 250 ml diluted blackcurrant juice
- ✔ 500 ml fizzy water
- ✔ ice cubes

1 Wash the strawberries, put them in a large bowl, add the sugar and the apple juice. Cover the bowl and leave it at room temperature for a couple of hours.

2 Shortly before serving, add the blackcurrant juice and lemon juice. Stir and add the fizzy water. Ladle the punch into glasses, add ice cubes, a twist of lemon peel and a sprig of strawberry leaves.

Japanese tea

According to an ancient legend, tea was discovered by a Chinese emperor around 2700 BC. Leaves from a wild tea bush fell into his pot of boiling water, and the emperor liked the taste of the new brew. Today the best tea comes from the mountain slopes of countries with lots of sun and rain. The tea bushes grow slowly and give more flavour. India and China produce most of the world's tea. Much of this is black tea, so called because the leaves turn black after being dried in ovens. The Japanese prefer green tea, made from leaves that are steamed and dried quickly. This tea is light green and has a delicate flavour. In Japan there is an ancient custom of entertaining friends in a formal tea ceremony. The hostess makes the tea according to traditional rules. The guest eats a sweet, sips the fragrant tea, and admires the beauty of the cup. Many Japanese girls are still taught how to perform this beautiful ceremony properly.

Halloween Horrors

To make horror faces for a haunting Halloween, ice your own fiendishly mouthwatering cakes.

YOU WILL NEED:

Cake Mixture
- ✔ plastic bowl   ✔ plastic bag   ✔ 225 g digestive biscuits
- ✔ 150 g caster sugar   ✔ 2 tablespoons cocoa powder
- ✔ 4 tablespoons ground almonds   ✔ rolling pin
- ✔ 75 g butter (or margarine)   ✔ 1 or 2 tablespoons milk

Butter Icing
- ✔ 100 g margarine   ✔ 250 g icing sugar   ✔ wooden spoon
- ✔ blue, green and red food colouring   ✔ bowls   ✔ metal spoon

To decorate
- ✔ liquorice sweets and strips   ✔ small sweets   ✔ strawberry laces

1 Put the biscuits in a plastic bag. Close the bag, and crush the biscuits with the end of a rolling pin.

2 Pour the biscuit crumbs into a bowl and mix them with the sugar, cocoa powder and ground almonds.

3 Soften the butter and pour it into the mixture. Add a little milk, so that the mixture is smooth but firm enough to shape. Divide the mixture into ten pieces, form them into balls, and then flatten them into 3-cm thick round cakes. Let them set in the fridge while you prepare the butter icing.

4 Put the margarine in a bowl and beat it with a wooden spoon until it is soft. Sift the icing sugar and add it in small amounts, beating well until the mixture is smooth. Divide it into three small bowls and add a few drops of different food colouring to each bowl. Use a metal spoon to mix in the colour, as a wooden spoon will stain.

5 Using the palette knife, cover the top of each cake with blue, green or red icing. Dip the knife in a mug of warm water when you are smoothing the icing, but leave the red icing rather rough.

6 Decorate your horrors with sweets, liquorice strips and strawberry laces. Press them into the icing for a really ghostly look.

Apple horrors

YOU WILL NEED:
- ✔ 4 apples ✔ 4 wooden skewers
- ✔ 100 g margarine ✔ 150 g icing sugar
- ✔ jelly beans ✔ blue food colouring
- ✔ liquorice sweets and strips

1 Wash and dry the apples before pushing a wooden skewer through each one.

3 Dip the apples into the bowl to coat them with icing. Then give your apple horrors jelly bean hair, a sweet nose and a liquorice ghoulish grin. Let them set in the fridge, and stand them in jam jars for serving.

2 Soften the margarine in a large bowl and add sifted icing sugar. When the mixture is smooth, mix in a few drops of blue food colouring.

Halloween customs

The Halloween festival on October 31 probably comes from an ancient Celtic new year festival. The Celts lived over 2,000 years ago in Britain, Ireland and northern France. On the last day of the old year the Druids, who were the priests and teachers of the Celts, lit huge bonfires to drive evil spirits away. To protect themselves further, the Druids offered the spirits good things to eat.

The autumn leaves, corn, apples and nuts that have become such a part of the Halloween season are reminders of the Druids' festival to celebrate harvest time. Today bobbing for apples is a favourite Halloween game. A large bowl is filled with water and apples are put in. The object of the game is to try and catch an apple in your mouth and take it out of the bowl, without using your hands. This sounds quite easy, but just try it!

Bird's Nests

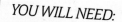

Here's how to make some birds and eggs to put in their nest. Make the birds and eggs a day before the nests, as they take about 24 hours to harden.

YOU WILL NEED:
- ✔ 2 tablespoons butter
- ✔ 1 tablespoon milk
- ✔ spoon
- ✔ juice and grated rind of 1 lemon
- ✔ 450 g icing sugar
- ✔ blue and yellow food colouring
- ✔ piece of card
- ✔ knife
- ✔ sugar balls
- ✔ bird-shaped cutter (optional)
- ✔ rolling pin
- ✔ saucepan
- ✔ 2 bowls
- ✔ scissors
- ✔ 12 cake cases
- ✔ 200 g cooking chocolate
- ✔ 1 tablespoon soft margarine
- ✔ 60 g shredded wheat
- ✔ water
- ✔ cling film

1 Melt and gently heat the butter, milk, grated lemon rind and two tablespoons of lemon juice in a pan. Do not boil.

2 When the mixture is cool, work in the icing sugar. If the mixture is too dry, add a few more drops of lemon juice.

3 Dust your work surface with icing sugar, and knead the mixture until it is a smooth, pliable dough.

4 Divide the mixture into two bowls and knead a few drops of food colouring into each mixture – blue in one, yellow in the other. If the mixture gets too moist, work in a little more icing sugar.

5 Cut out the birds with a bird cutter, or use this stencil. Copy the bird shape onto a piece of card 5 x 4 cm and cut it out. Roll out the blue icing to a thickness of 5 mm. Put the stencil on the icing and cut round it with a knife. Cut out four birds, adding a sugar ball for the birds' eyes. Use the rest of the blue icing to make small sugar eggs. Keep the dough wrapped in cling film when not in use.

6 Make some yellow birds and eggs in the same way, and then leave them to harden at room temperature.

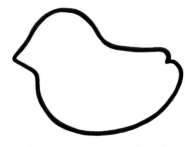

7 Melt the chocolate and margarine in a bowl by placing this over a small saucepan of hot water. Ask an adult to help.

8 Break the shredded wheat into small pieces and stir them in.

9 Spoon the mixture into the cake cases. Then decorate each nest with one of your birds and some eggs. Leave to set.

Why not make some of these bird's nests next Easter?

Wheat

People first grew wheat many thousands of years ago in the Middle East. In ancient Egypt, Greece and Rome, grain became such an important part of life that it was often used to pay taxes. Later wheat was grown all over Europe, and Spanish conquerors took it to Mexico in the 1520s. By the early seventeenth century, English settlers were growing wheat in America. Today the greatest producers of wheat are China, the former Soviet Union and the United States. It is fairly easy to grow wheat, which is usually planted with a machine called a seed drill. When the wheat is ripe, it is cut and separated using a combine harvester. There are many varieties of wheat, and two main types – common and durum wheat. Common, or bread, wheat is mainly grown to be milled into flour for baking. It is also used for breakfast cereals. Shredded wheat is made from toasted whole wheat. Durum wheat grows well in dry conditions and is used to make semolina and pasta such as spaghetti.

The Big Chill

You don't need an ice-cream machine to make these fabulous frozen treats.

1 Wash and hull the strawberries. Then put them in a large bowl, sprinkle on the icing sugar and mash them with a fork into a smooth pulp.

Strawberry scoop

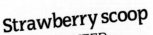

YOU WILL NEED:
- ✔ 500 g strawberries
- ✔ 1 tablespoon icing sugar
- ✔ 300 ml whipping cream
- ✔ 75 g sugar ✔ fork
- ✔ 125 g plain yoghurt
- ✔ silver foil ✔ large bowl
- ✔ whisk ✔ small pots
- ✔ jug ✔ plastic container
- ✔ lolly sticks

2 Whisk the cream in a jug until it is thick. Add the sugar and whisk until the cream forms stiff peaks.

3 Add the cream to the strawberry pulp, and put the mixture in a plastic container, covering it with silver foil. Put it in the freezer for an hour.

4 After an hour, beat the mixture with a fork to break up any ice crystals. Put it back in the freezer and do the same thing again an hour later. Strawberry ice cream takes up to three hours to freeze properly.

5 Cool off with a frozen yoghurt feast. Mix a tablespoon of the strawberry pulp with a teaspoon of sugar and the yoghurt. Fill small pots with the mixture and cover them with aluminium foil. Push lolly sticks through the foil tops before putting them in the freezer.

Lolly galore

YOU WILL NEED:
- ✔ 4 lolly moulds and sticks
- ✔ 150 ml orange squash
- ✔ 100 ml strawberry cordial
- ✔ ice tray   ✔ 1 lemon
- ✔ strawberries or other fruit (apple, peach, kiwi)
- ✔ water   ✔ cling film
- ✔ cocktail sticks

1 Push the lolly sticks halfway into the moulds. Pour 150 ml (a glass) of undiluted orange squash into a jug and add a squeeze of lemon. Make up another jug with 100 ml of strawberry cordial diluted with 50 ml of water. Half fill the moulds with orange or strawberry and put them in the freezer for an hour.

2 Cut two strawberries (or other fruit) into thin slices. Take the lollies out of the freezer, and arrange the fruit slices in the moulds, leaving enough space to cover the fruit with the rest of the juice. Put the moulds back in the freezer. After about an hour your lollies will be ready to eat. Hold them under running water to remove them from the moulds.

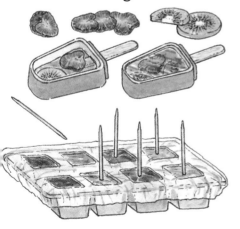

3 For an extra treat, make some mini lollies. You can use any fruit juice or cola drink. Just fill the sections of an ice tray with the drink and cover it with cling film. Push a cocktail or lolly stick through the film into each section, and freeze for two hours.

History of ice cream

Ice cream may have first been made in China almost 5,000 years ago. It is said that 3,000 years later the Roman emperor Nero sent slaves to the mountains to bring back snow, which was then served with honey and fruit. The explorer Marco Polo supposedly tasted flavoured ices on his travels through Asia, and took the recipes back to Italy in 1295. There are certainly references in books to ices being sold on the streets of Naples by 1690. A New York newspaper advertised an ice-cream "tavern" in 1786, when it was still a very special dish. The ice-cream cone was invented at an American exhibition in 1904. One story is that when an ice-cream seller ran out of clean dishes, the person in the next booth gave him a waffle rolled into the shape of a cone. Ice cream was quickly put into it and the ice-cream cone was born!

Chocolate Surprise

YOU WILL NEED:
- ✔ 2 Swiss rolls ✔ 100 g ground almonds
- ✔ 1 teaspoon jam ✔ 1 egg ✔ milk
- ✔ 2 tablespoons cocoa powder ✔ spoon
- ✔ 1 teaspoon each vanilla and almond essence ✔ chocolate strands
- ✔ almond chips ✔ coconut coating
- ✔ 20 petit-four cases ✔ large bowl
- ✔ 3 saucers ✔ sweet wrappers
- ✔ empty chocolate box ✔ PVA glue
- ✔ ribbon ✔ empty cereal packet
- ✔ wrapping and tissue paper ✔ scissors
- ✔ water ✔ brush ✔ old magazines

1 Crumble the Swiss rolls into a large bowl. Add the almonds, jam, cocoa powder and essences.

2 Separate the egg and add the yolk to the mixture. Keep the egg white in a separate bowl – you will need it later. Mix all the ingredients until the mixture is smooth and creamy. Add a drop of milk if it is too dry.

3 Divide the mixture into about twenty portions, and roll them into small balls.

4 Put the chocolate strands, almond chips and coconut coating into separate saucers. Dip the balls first in egg white, then in one of the three coatings, and place them in petit-four cases.

5 To gift-wrap your truffles, stick sweet wrappers or magazine cut-outs onto an empty chocolate box. Cover the whole box and then varnish it with PVA glue diluted with a little water. Make sure the box is completely dry before filling it with chocolate truffles and tying it with ribbon.

6 Or you could make a basket for your truffles. Coat an empty cereal packet with glue, and then cover it with wrapping paper. Draw a zigzag line all around the packet, leaving 4 cm on each side for the handle. Cut away the shaded part, overlap the two handle strips and glue them together. Put tissue paper at the bottom of the basket and put the truffles in. They are so delicious, they won't stay there long!

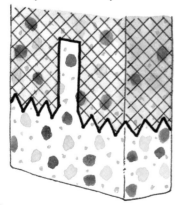

Chocolate

When the Spanish conqueror Hernan Cortes defeated the Aztecs in 1521, he found the Mexican Indians using cacao beans to make a drink. They called this *xocolatl*, and it was the favourite drink of the Aztec emperor, Montezuma. Cortes took cacao beans back to Spain, where chocolate became the special drink of rich aristocrats. The Spaniards sweetened it with sugar and tried adding new flavours, such as cinnamon and other spices. Three hundred years later a Dutchman named Van Houten invented a press that squeezed the rich cocoa butter out of cacao beans. This was then moulded into bars, and people began to eat chocolate as well as drinking it. It was still coarse and bitter, but in 1876 a Swiss manufacturer put milk into his chocolate and produced a new flavour. Further refinements have produced the smooth, velvety chocolate we know today. But it still all begins with the seeds of the cacao tree.

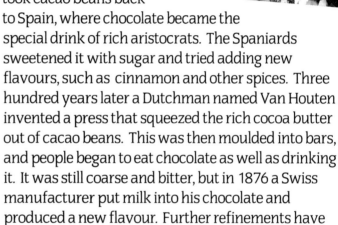

Express Cake

MESSY ACTIVITY

To catch this cake, ...

YOU WILL NEED:
- ✔ *450 g oblong Madeira cake*   ✔ *2 eggs*
- ✔ *600 g icing sugar*   ✔ *chocolate Swiss roll*
- ✔ *red, yellow, black and green food colouring*
- ✔ *4 tablespoons butter*   ✔ *icing bag and small nozzle*   ✔ *liquorice allsorts and wheels*
- ✔ *sweets*   ✔ *knife*   ✔ *wire rack*   ✔ *bowls*
- ✔ *whisk*   ✔ *tablespoon*   ✔ *palette knife*
- ✔ *sieve*   ✔ *cake board*   ✔ *wooden spoon*
- *instant sugar paste (optional)*

1 Cut a 2 cm thick slice from the base of the Madeira cake and place it on a wire rack to form the base for the locomotive boiler. Cut the rest of the cake in two widthways, as shown.

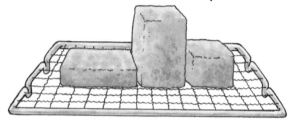

2 Stand the larger piece upright behind the base, for the cab, and the smaller piece behind the cab, to form the tender.

3 Now make some red icing to coat the cake. Crack the eggs and separate the whites from the yolks. Beat the egg whites in a bowl until frothy. Sift 400 g icing sugar and whisk it into the egg white a tablespoon at a time. Beat for about 10 minutes until the icing is soft and forms peaks. Then add some red food colouring drop by drop. You might have to add more sugar if it gets too sticky.

4 Use a palette knife to spread on the icing. Coat the top and sides of the base, cab and tender, and leave them to set for at least eight hours.

5 When the icing is hard, put the three pieces together on a board. Then put the Swiss roll on top of the base to form the boiler. Now you can join and decorate the locomotive with butter icing.

6 Beat the butter with a wooden spoon until it is soft. Add (150 g) sifted icing sugar in small amounts. Divide the mixture into small bowls and add different colouring to each one.

7 Using a small nozzle in an icing bag, decorate the edges of the locomotive covering up the joins as you go. Write a number on the cab.

8 If you don't want to make your own icing, you can use instant sugar paste. The piping tubes give different colours and are ideal for express decorators.

9 Add some liquorice wheels, a chimney and a window, and put sweets on top of the tender.

European cakes

Roman honey cake and medieval sweet cakes were the sponge and iced cakes of today. Some cake recipes have been around for thousands of years. The ancient Romans created cheesecake, using a cheese similar to the Italian ricotta we know today – a soft white cheese made from sheep's milk. Today cheesecake can be found on restaurant menus and supermarket shelves around the world. During the 1800s, cakes became real creations. The French and Austrians made such wonderful desserts that people travelled to Paris and Vienna just to taste them. The Sachertorte is named after a famous Viennese hotel-manager of the nineteenth century. This rich chocolate cake is almost the national dish of Austria. In France the traditional Christmas cake is a chocolate log, while in Italy it is the panettone –a light spiced breadlike cake. Cakes are made from similar recipes around the world, but local variations make them all the more interesting to taste!

Now hurry to catch the express before it's gone!

Tofu Spread

1 First make some tofu in your own press. Put a sieve over a mixing bowl and line it with a clean piece of cloth – muslin is best. Find a plate that fits into the sieve to act as a lid, and three or four weights.

YOU WILL NEED:
- ✔ metal sieve ✔ mixing bowl ✔ muslin cloth ✔ plate
- ✔ weights ✔ 2 tablespoons concentrated lemon juice
- ✔ warm water ✔ 250 ml soya milk ✔ small saucepan
- ✔ ladle ✔ 1 carrot ✔ celery ✔ cucumber ✔ parsley
- ✔ grater ✔ spoon

2 Mix the concentrated lemon juice with 50 ml of warm water.

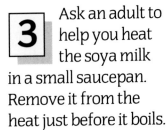

3 Ask an adult to help you heat the soya milk in a small saucepan. Remove it from the heat just before it boils.

4 Quickly stir the milk, and while it is swirling around, drip half the lemon mixture over the back of a spoon into it. Try to cover the whole surface of the milk.

5 Slowly stir the milk five times all around the saucepan, touching the bottom and sides with your spoon. Cover the saucepan and leave it to cool for three minutes.

6 Trickle the remaining lemon mixture over the back of a spoon into the centre and outer edges of the milk. The milk will now start to curdle. Gently stir it three or four times around the sides and the surface. Then cover the saucepan and leave for another six minutes.

7 When you uncover the milk, you will find that it has curdled. The white parts are the curds, and the yellow fluid is whey. To squeeze the whey from the curds, ladle the curdled milk into the cloth-lined sieve in your tofu press. Wrap the cloth over the mixture and put the lid and the weights on top. Leave for 40 minutes.

8 Then press the lid down firmly to make sure all the whey has been pressed out. You will be left with a lump of tofu, which you can shape into a bar and keep in a bowl of cold water in the fridge for up to a week. Change the water daily.

9 Now you can make a delicious tofu spread. Grate the carrot, celery and some cucumber, and add a tablespoon of chopped parsley. Mix all the ingredients into the tofu and blend it into a smooth spread.

Soya beans

Soya beans have been grown in China and Japan for thousands of years. The soya-bean plant grows to about one metre in height. It produces pods, each of which usually contains two or three beans, or seeds. Soya beans are highly nutritious. Because they contain so much protein, many East Asian people use them in the way that meat and eggs are used in Western countries. In East Asia people eat soya paste, sauce, milk, cheese, sprouts and curd. Tofu is the Japanese word for soya-bean curd, which is made from soya milk. Soya beans are pulped, heated and sieved to extract soya milk. In the East, tofu shops are as common as bakers in the West. Tofu makers rise at dawn to prepare fresh produce daily. Some families eat tofu three times a day. In recent years it has caught on in Europe and America among health-food eaters and lovers of Oriental food. And now you can make your own!

Food for Energy

All living things need energy to stay alive. For human beings that energy comes from the food we eat. Our bodies need nutrients for growth as well as for energy. There are several groups of nutrients

Carbohydrates

These are an important source of energy and include sugars and starches. Bread, potatoes, pasta and rice contain a lot of carbohydrate.

Proteins

These are essential to build and maintain healthy bones, muscles and skin; to ensure chemical reactions take place and to help protect against disease. Good sources include meat, fish, eggs, nuts, beans and cheese.

Fats

Fats are full of energy and carry important vitamins, but eating too many fatty foods is unhealthy. Fats are found in meat, dairy products and nuts.

Minerals

We need only small amounts of minerals each day, for growth and maintenance and to take part in chemical reactions in the body. Two important minerals are calcium and iron. Calcium is found in milk and whole-wheat bread, and iron in meat and eggs.

Bread and cereals
Bread, cereals, maize, pasta, potatoes.

Dairy products
Milk, cheese, yoghurt.

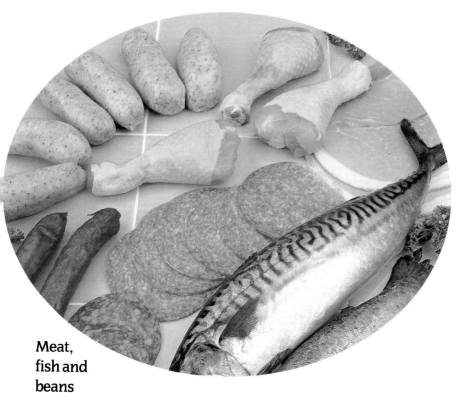

**Meat,
fish and
beans**
Red meat, fish, beans, poultry, eggs, nuts.

**Vegetables
and fruit**
Vegetables, fruit.

Vitamins
These are needed by body cells and to regulate body processes. Vitamin C, for example, is used in many processes and is found in citrus fruits and some vegetables.

Fibre
Fibre helps other foods pass easily through the digestive system. Good sources are wholemeal bread, brown rice and wholegrain pasta, as well as beans, vegetables and fruit.

Water
The body uses water in several ways. It is part of the blood, it helps keep our bodies cool when we sweat, and it carries wastes out of the body in urine. Water is present in other liquids and in various amounts in solid foods.

Healthy eating
Most foods contain several nutrients. Bread, for example, is rich in carbohydrates, protein and some minerals. Foods that are rich in nutrients can be grouped together in four basic food groups. It is important for good health to have a balanced diet by eating a variety of foods from all these groups.

Glossary

Aztecs - Mexican Indians whose empire was destroyed by Spanish conquerors in the early 16th century.

blend - to mix together.

bran - the outer protective layer of a grain.

cacao - a tropical tree whose seeds are used to make cocoa and chocolate.

cereals - grasses that produce edible grains.

cinnamon - a spice obtained from the bark of the cinnamon tree.

combine harvester - a machine that cuts, threshes and cleans cereals such as wheat.

curd - a semi-solid substance formed by adding acid to milk.

curdle - to turn into curd.

desiccated - dried.

dessert - a sweet course at the end of a meal.

diet - the food and drink that a person regularly has.

dilute - to make weaker by adding water.

fibre - a substance that helps other foods pass easily through the body's digestive system.

grain - the seed of a cereal plant.

grate - to rub (on a grater) to make into small shreds.

Halloween - a festival on October 31, the eve of All Saints' Day.

hull - to remove the outer covering of a fruit.

ingredient - an item of food listed in a recipe.

knead - to work and press into a mixture with your hands.

minerals - substances in food that are needed for growth and maintenance of the body and to take part in chemical reactions in the body.

muesli - a mixture of oats, nuts and fruit eaten with milk.

muslin - a fine cotton fabric.

nutrient - a substance that gives life and growth.

nutritious - nourishing, giving life and growth.

petit four - a small sweet cake.

pith - the tissue lining the inside of the rind of fruit.

protein - substances that are essential for building and maintaining the body, for chemical reactions, and to protect against disease.

punch - a mixed drink containing fruit juice.

rind - the outer layer of a fruit, cheese or bacon.

score - to make cuts in.

seed drill - a machine for planting seeds.

skewer - a long pin for holding food in position.

tofu - soya-bean curd, made from soya milk.

vanilla - a flavouring extract

Useful Websites

www.kidshealth.org/kid
is a fun and informative website and includes recipes, such as 'Ants on a Log' and 'Perfect Peachy Freeze'! It also covers a range of health issues, from looking at what vitamins and minerals do, to discussing how to eat healthily, like an athlete.

www.bbc.co.uk/cbbc/ bluepeter/active/bakes
is full of fun and tasty recipes, ranging from 'Breakfast Bonanza Smoothies' to 'Moroccan Pastilla'!

www.nutritionexplorati ons.org/kids
is an educational website. It is packed with information, presented through interactive games, activites and quizzes. It also includes competitions and recipes.

www.bbc.co.uk/kent/ food/kids/
is another great website, packed with easy-to-follow recipes for kids, including food from the main food groups.

Places to visit
United Kingdom

The Science Museum
Exhibition Road
South Kensington
London SW7 2DD
www.sciencemuseum. org.uk

Australia

Queensland Science Centre
Queensland Museum
Southbank
Queensland
www.qmuseum.qld. gov.au

Index

Additional Photographs:
Zefa Picture Library 9, 13, 15, 17, 19, 20, 23, 27, cover; Robert Harding 7, 11, 25